Contents

Some words are in bold, **like this**. You can find them in the glossary on page 23.

What is a jaguar?

A jaguar is a **mammal**.

Many mammals have hairy bodies and feed their babies milk.

tiger

Jaguars belong to a group of mammals called big cats.

Tigers are another type of big cat.

What do jaguars look like?

Jaguars have strong bodies with short, thick tails.

They have large heads, with strong **jaws** and sharp teeth.

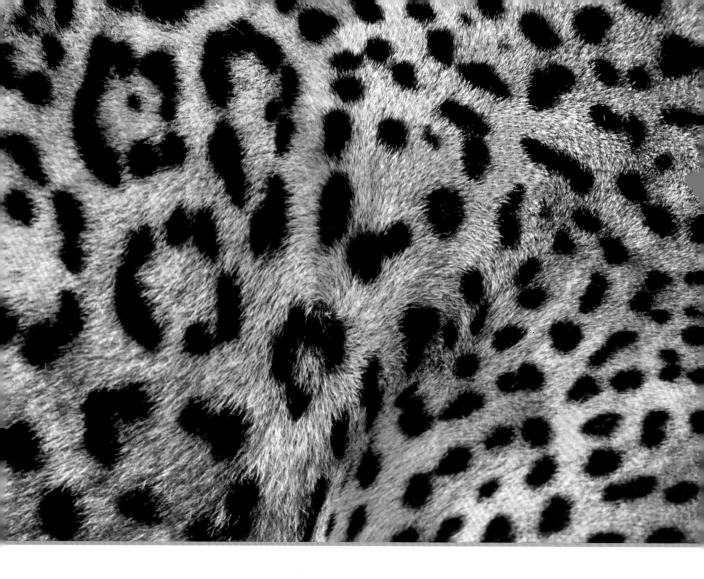

Most jaguars have light, golden-brown fur covered with black spots.

A few jaguars have very dark fur and look almost black.

Where do jaguars live?

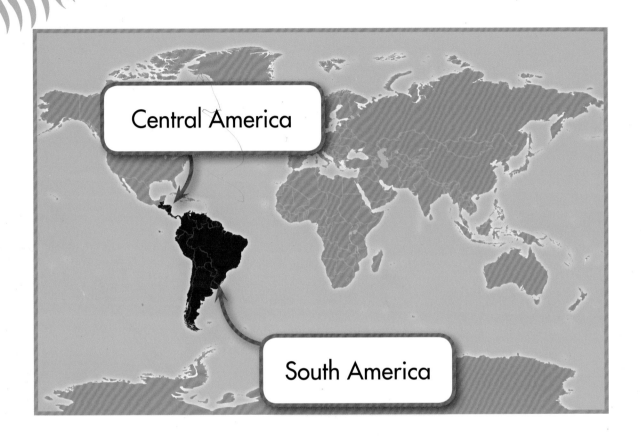

Central America

South America

Jaguars live in the **rainforests** of Central America and South America.

It is warm and wet in the rainforest all the year round.

Jaguars live near rivers and **swamps**.

They hunt for food in the water and on land.

What do jaguars do in the evening?

In the evening, jaguars start hunting.

A jaguar may carry on hunting
all night.

Jaguars have special eyes that can see in dim light.

This helps the jaguars to find their **prey** at night.

How do jaguars catch their food?

At night, jaguars hunt for **prey** in the forest.

A jaguar hides among the trees and then suddenly it pounces.

jaws

The jaguar has very strong **jaws** and sharp teeth for catching its prey.

It can kill an animal by biting right through its **skull**.

What do jaguars eat?

deer

Jaguars hunt many other **rainforest** animals.

Some of these are large animals, such as deer and wild pigs.

turtle

Jaguars also catch **prey** in the water, such as fish, frogs, and turtles.

Their teeth are sharp enough to bite through a turtle's shell.

Do jaguars live in groups?

Jaguars live on their own.

Each jaguar roars loudly to keep other jaguars away from its patch of forest.

cub

Jaguars only meet up when they are ready to have **cubs**.

Jaguar cubs live with their mother for up to two years, learning how to hunt.

What do jaguars do in the morning?

In the morning, a jaguar goes out hunting.

Many **rainforest** animals are just waking up, so there is plenty of **prey** around.

Sometimes, a jaguar stops by the water's edge.

It waits for an animal to come for a drink, then it leaps on to its prey from behind.

What do jaguars do in the day?

After hunting, a jaguar spends most of the day resting or sleeping.

A jaguar sleeps for about 12 hours a day.

Sometimes jaguars rest in caves by the riverbank.

Sometimes they climb **rainforest** trees and go to sleep in the branches.

jaguar body map

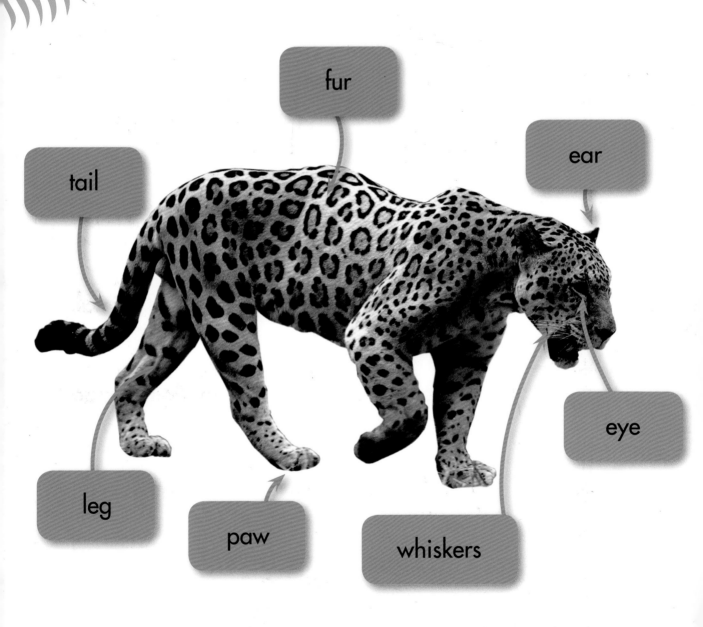

fur

ear

tail

eye

leg

paw

whiskers

Glossary

 **cub** baby jaguar

 **jaws** top and bottom parts of the mouth

 **mammal** animal that feeds its babies milk. Most mammals have hair or fur.

 **prey** animal that is hunted by other animals for food

 **rainforest** thick forest with very tall trees and a lot of rain

 **skull** bony part of the head that contains the brain

 **swamp** wet, muddy land

Find out more

Books

Rainforest Animals (Focus on Habitats), Stephen Savage
  (Wayland, 2006)
Usborne Beginners: Rainforest, Lucy Beckett-Bowman
  (Usborne, 2008)

Websites

http://kids.nationalgeographic.com/Animals/CreatureFeature/
  Jaguars
http://animal.discovery.com/mammals/jaguar/
http://a-z-animals.com/animals/jaguar/

Index